Pyramid Fractions

Fraction Multiplication and Division Workbook

A Fun Way to Practice Multiplying & Dividing Fractions

Chris McMullen, Ph.D.

Pyramid Fractions – Fraction Multiplication and Division Workbook: A Fun Way to Practice Multiplying and Dividing Fractions

Copyright © 2010 Chris McMullen, Ph.D.

All rights reserved. This includes the right to reproduce any portion of this book in any form. However, teachers who purchase one copy of this book, or borrow one physical copy from a library, may make and distribute photocopies of selected pages for instructional purposes for their own classes only. Also, parents who purchase one copy of this book, or borrow one physical copy from a library, may make and distribute photocopies of selected pages for use by their own children only.

CreateSpace

Nonfiction / Education / Elementary School / Mathematics
Children's / Science / Mathematics / Fractions

ISBN: 1456510886

EAN-13: 978-1456510886

Contents

Introduction	2
How to Multiply Fractions	3
Practice Multiplying Fractions	5
How to Divide Fractions	22
Practice Dividing Fractions	23
Answers	40

Introduction

    These fraction problems are presented in a creative visual pattern. The idea behind these pyramid fraction problems is for the novelty to engage the interest of young students (and perhaps even some teachers and parents, too). This layout also promotes the development of useful visual skills, too. In this way, students can improve their math fluency and also enjoy doing the math. This format of practicing also ties into a major pedagogical method that has proven teaching effectiveness – visual strategies for learning.

    Here is how pyramid math works. There are 15 bricks stacked in a pyramid formation. The 5 bricks in the longest row are filled with fractions. For multiplication: Start at the second row from the bottom; in each brick, enter the product of the fractions from the two bricks below it; work your way up to the top of the pyramid. Division works very much the same, except: The pyramid is up-side-down, so you work downward instead of upward; and you always divide the left fraction by the right fraction (from the two bricks above).

    The rectangles surrounding the pyramid provide workspace for all of the solutions. The workspaces and answers are all numbered for easy correspondence. The answers to all of the problems are tabulated at the back of the book. The first exercise is partially completed and annotated with instructions in order to help you get started. There are also two completely answered problems on the cover.

    May everyone enjoy pyramid fractions! ☺

A Fun Way to Practice Multiplying and Dividing Fractions

How to Multiply Fractions

Mixed Numbers and Improper Fractions

If you want to convert a mixed number to an improper fraction, follow these steps:
1. Multiply the denominator of the mixed number by the whole number out front.
2. Add the numerator of the mixed number to the product you obtained in Step 1.
3. Write your answer from Step 2 over the denominator from the mixed number.

EXAMPLES

$$3\frac{2}{5} = \frac{5 \times 3 + 2}{5} = \frac{15 + 2}{5} = \frac{\mathbf{17}}{\mathbf{5}} \quad , \quad 5\frac{3}{8} = \frac{8 \times 5 + 3}{8} = \frac{40 + 3}{8} = \frac{\mathbf{43}}{\mathbf{8}}$$

If you want to convert an improper fraction to a mixed number, follow these steps:
1. Divide the numerator by the denominator using long division.
2. The integer part of the quotient equals the integer part of the mixed number.
3. To get the fractional part, place the remainder over the denominator.

EXAMPLES

$$\frac{13}{4} = 13 \div 4 = 3\text{R}1 = 3\frac{\mathbf{1}}{\mathbf{4}} \quad , \quad \frac{5}{3} = 5 \div 3 = 1\text{R}2 = 1\frac{\mathbf{2}}{\mathbf{3}} \quad , \quad \frac{19}{8} = 19 \div 8 = 2\text{R}3 = 2\frac{\mathbf{3}}{\mathbf{8}}$$

Greatest Common Factor

The **greatest common factor** among two whole numbers is the largest whole number that evenly divides into both of the numbers. For example, the greatest common factor of 12 and 18 is 6: $12 = 6 \times 2$ and $18 = 6 \times 3$.

EXAMPLES

The greatest common factor of 8 and 20 is **4**: $8 = 4 \times 2$ and $20 = 4 \times 5$.
The greatest common factor of 15 and 25 is **5**: $15 = 5 \times 3$ and $25 = 5 \times 5$.
The greatest common factor of 54 and 72 is **18**: $54 = 18 \times 3$ and $72 = 18 \times 4$.

Reduced Fractions

A proper or improper fraction can be **reduced** if the numerator and denominator share a common factor. To reduce a proper or improper fraction, divide both the numerator and denominator by their greatest common factor.

EXAMPLES

$$\frac{9}{6} = \frac{9 \div 3}{6 \div 3} = \frac{3}{2} \quad , \quad \frac{8}{32} = \frac{8 \div 8}{32 \div 8} = \frac{1}{4} \quad , \quad \frac{36}{27} = \frac{36 \div 9}{27 \div 9} = \frac{4}{3} \quad , \quad \frac{14}{35} = \frac{14 \div 7}{35 \div 7} = \frac{2}{5}$$

Multiplying Fractions

To multiply two proper and/or improper fractions together, simply multiply their numerators together and multiply their denominators together. If your answer is reducible, reduce it.

EXAMPLES

$$\frac{3}{4} \times \frac{5}{8} = \frac{15}{32}$$

$$\frac{2}{3} \times \frac{6}{5} = \frac{12}{15} = \frac{12 \div 3}{15 \div 3} = \frac{4}{5}$$

It is sometimes more efficient to reduce the fraction before multiplying the numbers together in the numerator and denominator. In the example above, the 2 times 6 divided by 3 times 5 can be reduced to 2 times 2 divided by 1 times 5, giving the reduced answer of 4/5 more readily. The point is that it is simpler to cancel the greatest common factor before multiplying the numbers together in the numerator and denominator.

A Fun Way to Practice Multiplying and Dividing Fractions

❽

❾

❿

On this page, we did exercises 1, 2, and 5 to serve as examples.

Start at the bottom row (exercises 1 thru 4) and work your way up the pyramid.

❺ $\frac{1}{2} \times \frac{3}{8} = \frac{3}{16}$

MULTIPLICATION

❻

In exercise 5, we multiplied 1/2 by 3/8 to get 3/16.

In exercise 6, multiply 3/8 by your answer to exercise 3.

Write your answers in the numbered bricks in the pyramid and show your work in the corresponding numbered workspaces.

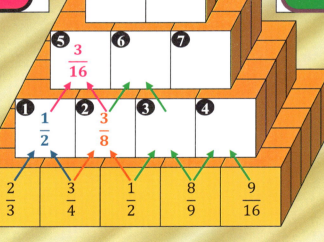

❼

❶ $\frac{2}{3} \times \frac{3}{4} = \frac{2}{4} = \frac{1}{2}$

In exercise 1, we multiplied 2/3 by 3/4 to get 1/2.

❷ $\frac{3}{4} \times \frac{1}{2} = \frac{3}{8}$

In exercise 2, we multiplied 3/4 by 1/2 to get 3/8.

❸ In exercise 3, multiply 1/2 by 8/9.

❹ In exercise 4, multiply 8/9 by 9/16.

Check your answers at the back of the book to make sure that you are solving the problems correctly.

Pyramid Fractions – Fraction Multiplication and Division Workbook

A Fun Way to Practice Multiplying and Dividing Fractions

Pyramid Fractions – Fraction Multiplication and Division Workbook

A Fun Way to Practice Multiplying and Dividing Fractions

Pyramid Fractions – Fraction Multiplication and Division Workbook

A Fun Way to Practice Multiplying and Dividing Fractions

Pyramid Fractions – Fraction Multiplication and Division Workbook

A Fun Way to Practice Multiplying and Dividing Fractions

Pyramid Fractions – Fraction Multiplication and Division Workbook

A Fun Way to Practice Multiplying and Dividing Fractions

Pyramid Fractions – Fraction Multiplication and Division Workbook

A Fun Way to Practice Multiplying and Dividing Fractions

Pyramid Fractions – Fraction Multiplication and Division Workbook

A Fun Way to Practice Multiplying and Dividing Fractions

Pyramid Fractions – Fraction Multiplication and Division Workbook

A Fun Way to Practice Multiplying and Dividing Fractions

How to Divide Fractions

Reciprocals

To find the **reciprocal** of a proper fraction or an improper fraction, simply swap the numerator and denominator. For example, the reciprocal of $\frac{3}{4}$ is $\frac{4}{3}$. To find the reciprocal of a whole number, just divide one by the whole number. For example, the reciprocal of 3 is $\frac{1}{3}$. To find the reciprocal of a mixed number, first convert the mixed number to an improper fraction.

EXAMPLES

The reciprocal of $\frac{12}{5}$ is $\frac{5}{12}$. The reciprocal of $\frac{3}{7}$ is $\frac{7}{3}$. The reciprocal of $1\frac{1}{4}$ is $\frac{4}{5}$ (since $1\frac{1}{4} = \frac{5}{4}$). The reciprocal of 4 is $\frac{1}{4}$. The reciprocal of $\frac{1}{2}$ is **2** (since $\frac{2}{1} = 2$).

Dividing Fractions

To divide two fractions, first find the reciprocal of the second fraction (i.e. the divisor) and then multiply the first fraction with the reciprocal of the second fraction. If your answer is reducible, reduce it.

EXAMPLES

$$\frac{2}{3} \div \frac{6}{5} = \frac{2}{3} \times \frac{5}{6} = \frac{10}{18} = \frac{10 \div 3}{18 \div 3} = \frac{5}{9}$$

$$\frac{3}{4} \div \frac{5}{8} = \frac{3}{4} \times \frac{8}{5} = \frac{24}{20} = \frac{24 \div 4}{20 \div 4} = \frac{6}{5}$$

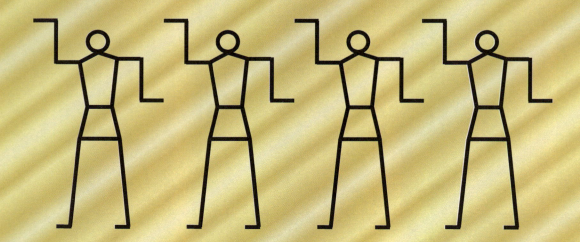

A Fun Way to Practice Multiplying and Dividing Fractions

❶
$$\frac{1}{2} \div \frac{1}{3} = \frac{1}{2} \times 3$$
$$= \frac{3}{2} = 1\frac{1}{2}$$

In exercise 1, we divided 1/2 by 1/3.

❷
$$\frac{1}{3} \div \frac{1}{6} = \frac{1}{3} \times 6$$
$$= \frac{6}{3} = 2$$

In exercise 2, we divided 1/3 by 1/6.

❸
In exercise 3, divide 1/6 by 1/12.

❹
In exercise 4, divide 1/12 by 1/4.

On this page, we did exercises 1, 2, and 5 to serve as examples.

Start at the top row (exercises 1 thru 4) and work your way down the pyramid.

❺
$$1\frac{1}{2} \div 2 = \frac{3}{2} \times \frac{1}{2} = \frac{3}{4}$$

In exercise 5, we divided 1-1/2 by 2.

❻
In exercise 6, divide 3/4 by your answer to exercise 3.

❼

Write your answers in the numbered bricks in the pyramid and show your work in the corresponding numbered workspaces.

❽

❾

❿

Always divide the fraction on the left by the fraction on the right.

Check your answers at the back of the book to make sure that you are solving the problems correctly.

DIVISION

Pyramid Fractions – Fraction Multiplication and Division Workbook

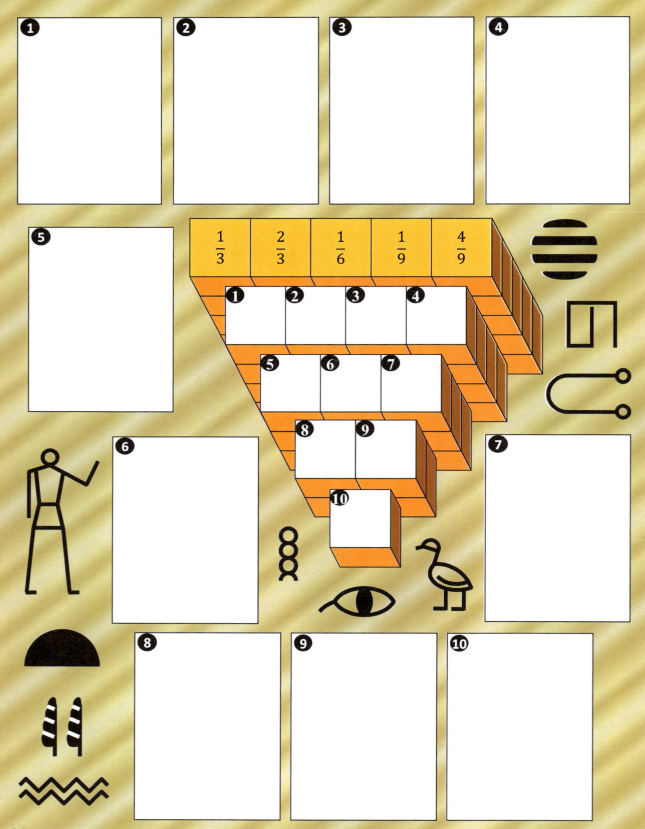

A Fun Way to Practice Multiplying and Dividing Fractions

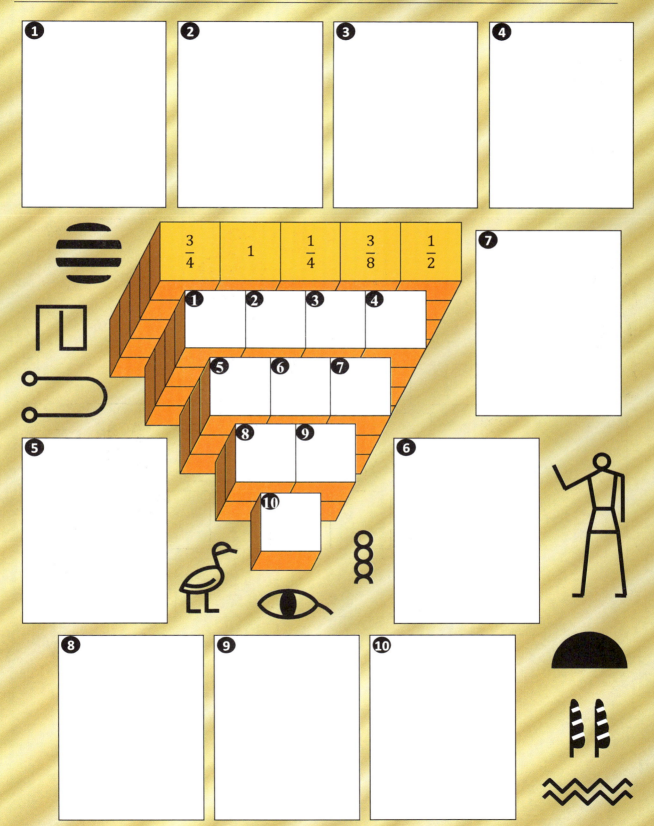

Pyramid Fractions – Fraction Multiplication and Division Workbook

A Fun Way to Practice Multiplying and Dividing Fractions

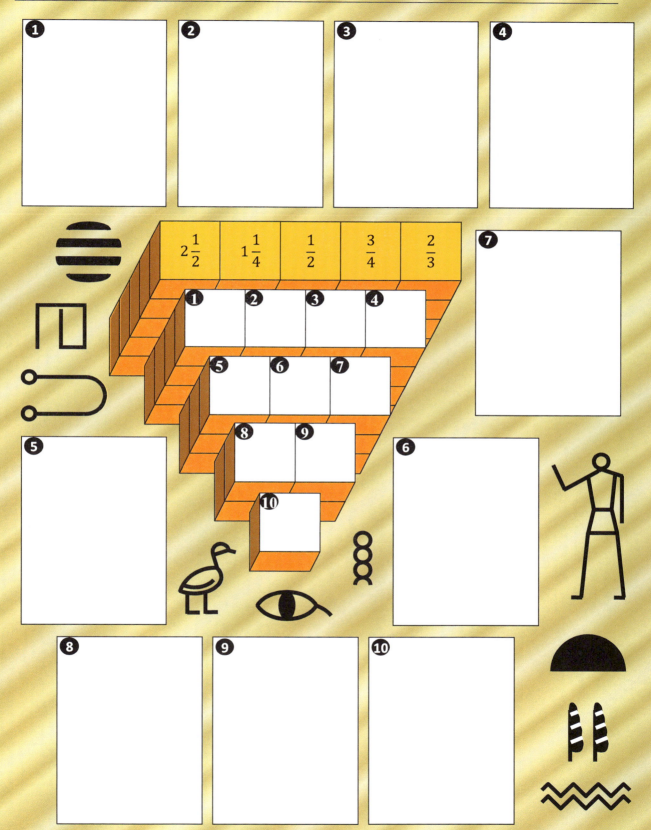

Pyramid Fractions – Fraction Multiplication and Division Workbook

A Fun Way to Practice Multiplying and Dividing Fractions

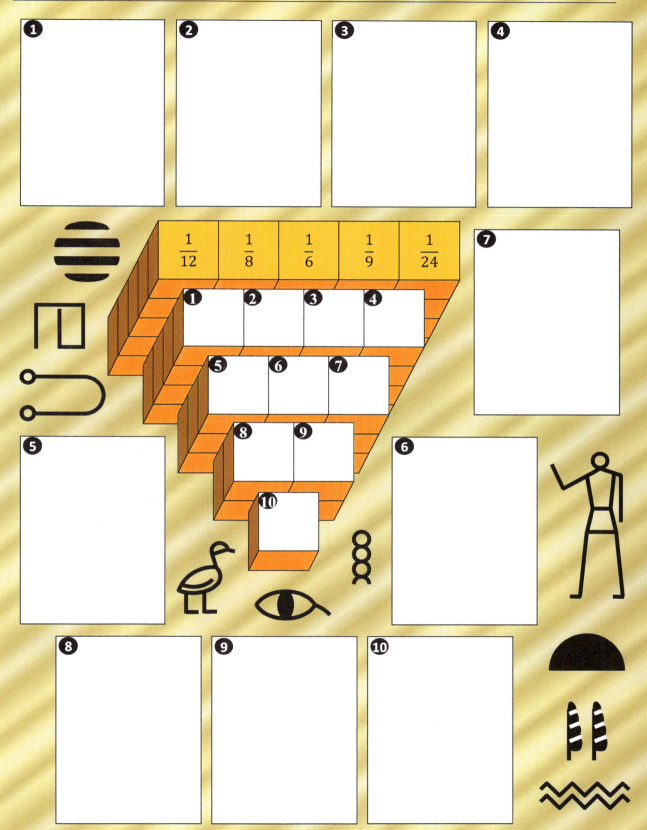

Pyramid Fractions – Fraction Multiplication and Division Workbook

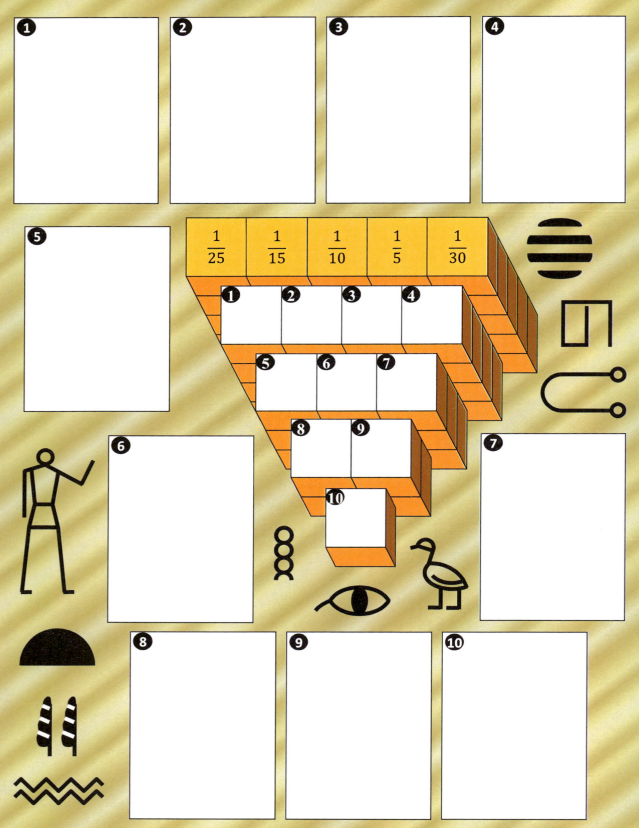

A Fun Way to Practice Multiplying and Dividing Fractions

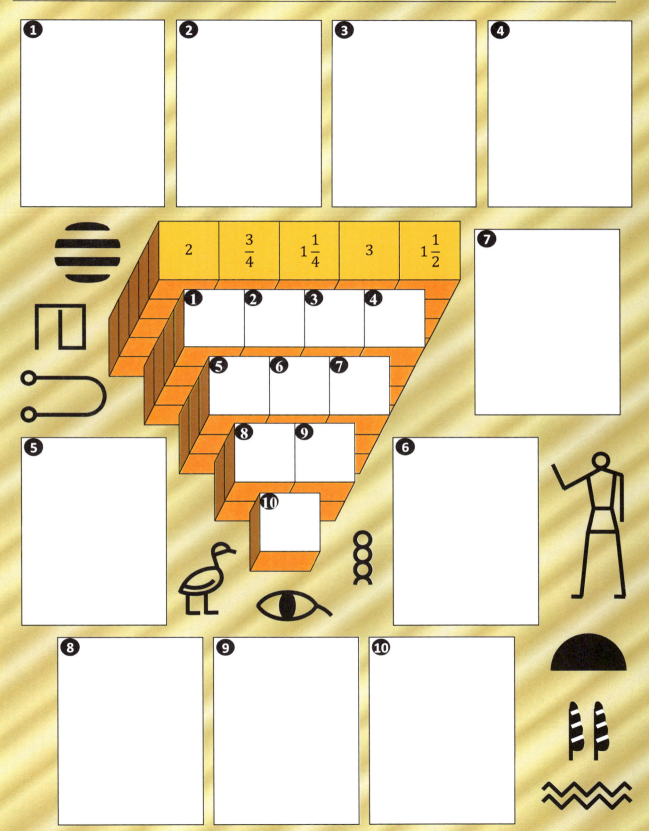

Pyramid Fractions – Fraction Multiplication and Division Workbook

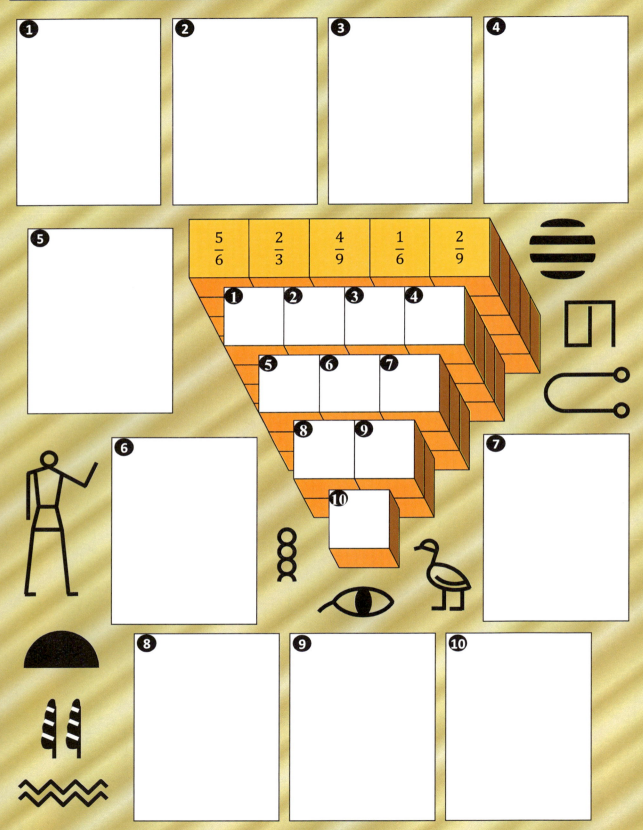

A Fun Way to Practice Multiplying and Dividing Fractions

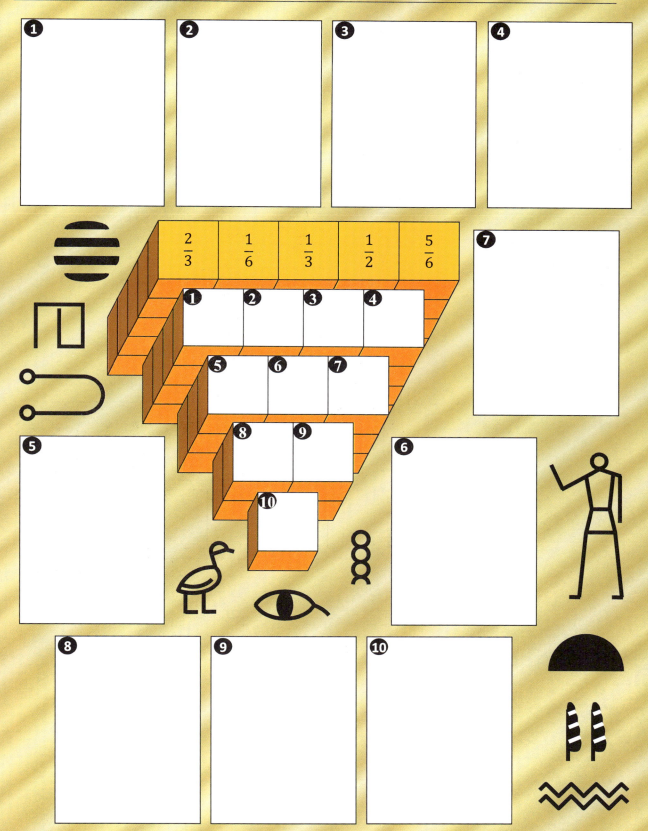

Pyramid Fractions – Fraction Multiplication and Division Workbook

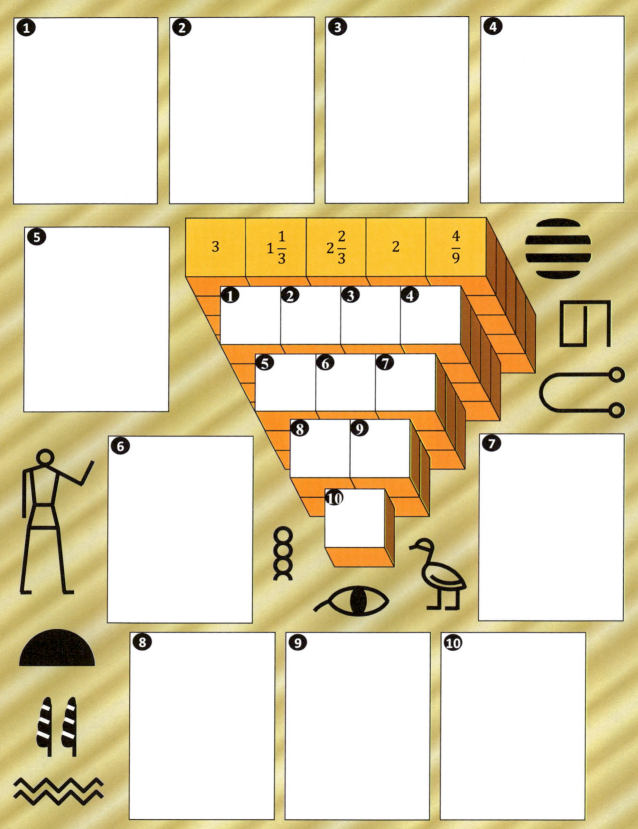

34

A Fun Way to Practice Multiplying and Dividing Fractions

Pyramid Fractions – Fraction Multiplication and Division Workbook

A Fun Way to Practice Multiplying and Dividing Fractions

Pyramid Fractions – Fraction Multiplication and Division Workbook

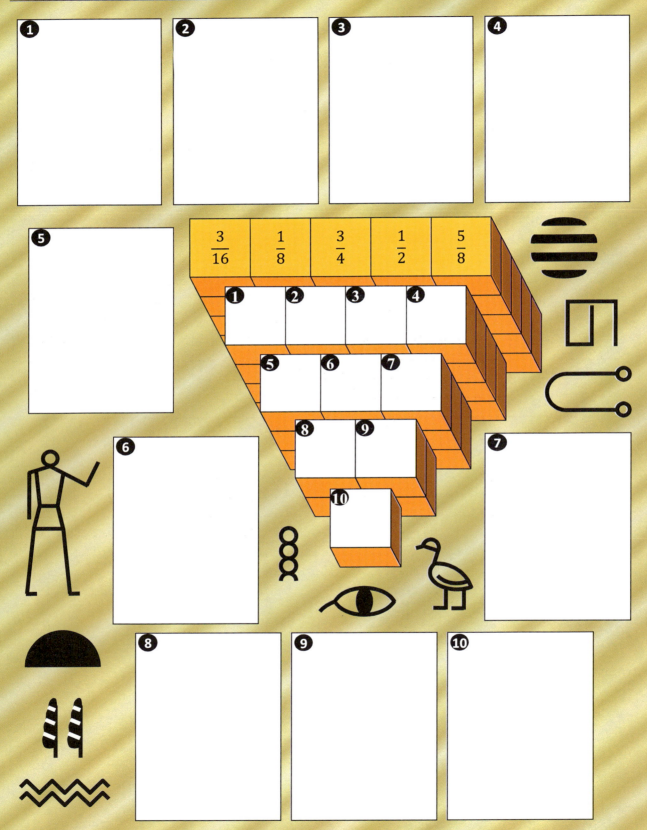

A Fun Way to Practice Multiplying and Dividing Fractions

Pyramid Fractions – Fraction Multiplication and Division Workbook

Multiplication Answers

Page 5	1/2	3/8	4/9	1/2	3/16	1/6	2/9	1/32	1/27	1/864
Page 6	4	3	1/2	1/6	12	1 1/2	1/12	18	1/8	2 1/4
Page 7	1/4	1	1 1/3	1/12	1/4	1 1/3	1/9	1/3	4/27	4/81
Page 8	1/3	1/2	3/5	2/3	1/6	3/10	2/5	1/20	3/25	3/500
Page 9	1/12	2/9	1 1/3	4 1/2	1/54	8/27	6	4/729	1 7/9	64/6561
Page 10	3/8	2 1/4	2/3	7/9	27/32	1 1/2	14/27	1 17/64	7/9	63/64
Page 11	4/9	1/3	1/2	1 1/2	4/27	1/6	3/4	2/81	1/8	1/324
Page 12	1/2	5/9	1/2	2/15	5/18	5/18	1/15	25/324	1/54	25/17496
Page 13	7/9	7/18	1/2	2	49/162	7/36	1	343/5832	7/36	2401/209952
Page 14	1	2/3	2/9	1/3	2/3	4/27	2/27	8/81	8/729	64/59049
Page 15	3/5	25/32	1/2	1 1/3	15/32	25/64	2/3	375/2048	25/96	9375/196608
Page 16	1	1/2	3/4	9/16	1/2	3/8	27/64	3/16	81/512	243/8192
Page 17	2/5	4	5/9	3/8	1 3/5	2 2/9	5/24	3 5/9	25/54	1 157/243
Page 18	1 1/2	3 1/3	2/3	1/2	5	2 2/9	1/3	11 1/9	20/27	8 56/243
Page 19	2 1/2	1 2/3	1 1/2	3/8	4 1/6	2 1/2	9/16	10 5/12	1 13/32	14 83/128
Page 20	6 7/8	3 3/4	2/3	1 7/18	25 25/32	2 1/2	25/27	64 29/64	2 17/54	149 227/1152
Page 21	1/2	1	7 1/9	1 1/2	1/2	7 1/9	10 2/3	3 5/9	75 23/27	242 68/81

Division Answers

Page 23	1 1/2	2	2	1/3	3/4	1	6	3/4	1/6	4 1/2
Page 24	1/2	4	1 1/2	1/4	1/8	2 2/3	6	3/64	4/9	27/256
Page 25	3/4	4	2/3	3/4	3/16	6	8/9	1/32	6 3/4	1/216
Page 26	1 1/3	1 1/3	2	1 1/8	1	2/3	1 7/9	1 1/2	3/8	4
Page 27	2	2 1/2	2/3	1 1/8	4/5	3 3/4	16/27	16/75	6 21/64	1024/30375
Page 28	4	3/4	1/6	12	5 1/3	4 1/2	1/72	1 5/27	324	8/2187
Page 29	2/3	3/4	1 1/2	2 2/3	8/9	1/2	9/16	1 7/9	8/9	2
Page 30	3/5	2/3	1/2	6	9/10	1 1/3	1/12	27/40	16	27/640
Page 31	2 2/3	3/5	5/12	2	4 4/9	1 11/25	5/24	3 7/81	6 114/125	15625/34992
Page 32	1 1/4	1 1/2	2 2/3	3/4	5/6	9/16	3 5/9	1 13/27	81/512	9 797/2187
Page 33	4	1/2	2/3	3/5	8	3/4	1 1/9	10 2/3	27/40	15 65/81
Page 34	2 1/4	1/2	1 1/3	4 1/2	4 1/2	3/8	8/27	12	1 17/64	9 13/27
Page 35	1 1/2	4/9	3	1 1/2	3 3/8	4/27	2	22 25/32	2/27	307 35/64
Page 36	1/8	2 2/3	2 1/4	3/4	3/64	1 5/27	3	81/2048	32/81	6561/65536
Page 37	3/4	1/6	3	4	4 1/2	1/18	3/4	81	2/27	1093 1/2
Page 38	1 1/2	1/6	1 1/2	4/5	9	1/9	1 7/8	81	8/135	1366 7/8
Page 39	2	4/9	3	3	4 1/2	4/27	1	30 3/8	4/27	205 1/32

Made in the USA
Lexington, KY
05 June 2011